Land of Liberty

West Virginia

W0006638

by Fran Hodgkins

Consultant:
Paul Rakes
Assistant History Professor
West Virginia University
Institute of Technology

Capstone
press
Mankato, Minnesota

Capstone Press
151 Good Counsel Drive • P.O. Box 669 • Mankato, Minnesota 56002
http://www.capstone-press.com

Library of Congress Cataloging-in-Publication Data
Hodgkins, Fran, 1964–
    West Virginia/by Fran Hodgkins.
    p. cm.—(Land of liberty)
    Includes bibliographical references and index.
    ISBN 0-7368-2205-4 (hardcover)
    1. West Virginia—Juvenile literature. [1. West Virginia.] I. Title. II. Series.
F241.3.H63 2004
975.4—dc21   2002154707

Summary: An introduction to the geography, history, government, politics, economy, resources, people, and culture of West Virginia, including maps, charts, and a recipe.

Editorial Credits
Carrie Braulick and Sarah L. Schuette, editors; Jennifer Schonborn, series designer; Linda Clavel, book designer; Enoch Peterson, illustrator; Eric Kudalis, product planning editor

Photo Credits
Cover images: Blackwater Falls State Park, Pat and Chuck Blackley; West Virginia landscape, PhotoDisc Inc.

Ann & Rob Simpson, 14, 47; AP/Wide World Photos, 4; Bill Beatty, 42–43: Blenko Glass Co., 41; Capstone Press/Gary Sundermeyer, 54; Corbis/Bettmann, 26, 29, 34, 50; Corbis/Macduff Everton, 38–39; Corbis/Reuters NewMedia Inc., 53; Folio Inc., 44; Folio Inc./David R. Frazier, 30; Harper's Weekly, 25; Image Ideas Inc., 56; North Wind Picture Archives, 16, 20; One Mile Up Inc., 55 (both); Pat & Chuck Blackley, 8, 12–13; PhotoDisc Inc., 57; Photri-Microstock/David Fattaleh, 48–49; Stock Montage Inc., 18, 23, 58; Transparencies Inc./Chris Ippolito, 63; Unicorn Stock Photos/Jean Higgins, 36; U.S. Postal Service, 59

Artistic Effects
Corbis, PhotoDisc Inc.

1 2 3 4 5 6 08 07 06 05 04 03

Table of Contents

Marble players from all over the country participate in the annual National Marbles Tournament sponsored by Marble King.

Chapter 1

About West Virginia

Marble King in Paden City, West Virginia, makes one million marbles each day. Sellers Peltier and Berry Pink opened the marble factory in St. Marys in 1949. Pink traveled around the United States giving away marbles. He hosted marble tournaments. Pink earned the nickname of "The Marble King." After a fire destroyed the first factory in 1958, Marble King moved to Paden City.

Today, Marble King is the country's largest maker of marbles. Many other marble factories also are located in West Virginia. The state is known as the marble capital of the United States.

"I suppose that if the more than one million mountains in West Virginia were leveled flat, the state would reach all the way to Texas."
— *Robert C. Byrd, U.S. Senator from West Virginia*

The Mountain State

West Virginia's nickname is the Mountain State. It is the only state that lies completely within the Appalachian Mountains. This range runs through the eastern United States from Georgia to Canada.

West Virginia is a southeastern state. Virginia lies along its eastern and southern borders. Kentucky and Ohio are to the west. Pennsylvania and Maryland border West Virginia to the north.

West Virginia is oddly shaped. Its borders are formed mainly by rivers. The northern and eastern parts of the state jut out. People say these parts of the state look like handles. The other part of the state looks like a cooking pot. For this reason, some people call West Virginia the Panhandle State.

West Virginia Cities

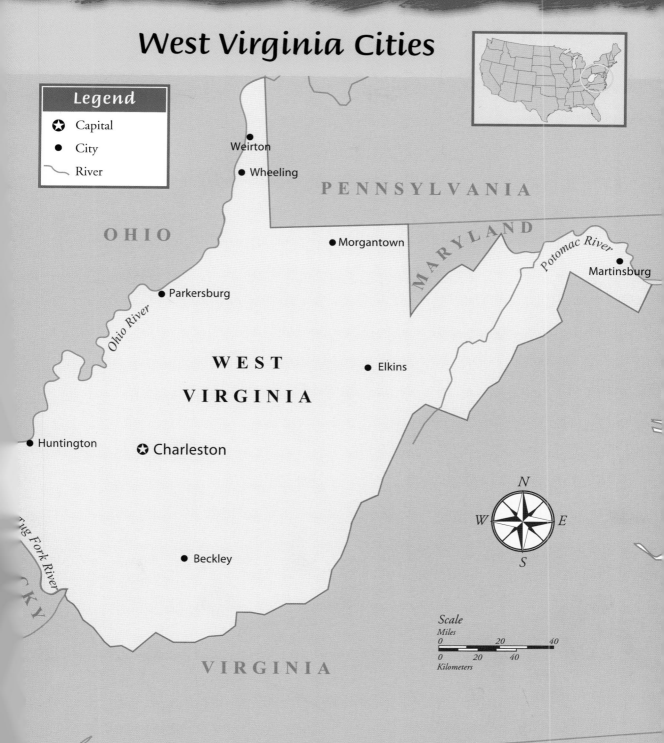

Legend

★ Capital

● City

〜 River

OHIO

PENNSYLVANIA

MARYLAND

Potomac River

● Weirton

● Wheeling

● Morgantown

● Martinsburg

● Parkersburg

Ohio River

**WEST
VIRGINIA**

● Elkins

● Huntington

★ Charleston

ug Fork River

CKY

● Beckley

VIRGINIA

N
W   E
S

Scale
Miles
0   20   40
0   20   40
Kilometers

The thickly forested Appalachian Ridge and Valley Region lies in the eastern part of West Virginia.

Chapter 2

Land, Climate, and Wildlife

West Virginia is one of the country's most rugged states. It has very few large, flat areas. Rolling hills cover the western part of the state. West Virginia's eastern and central parts are mountainous. West Virginia has the highest average elevation of any state east of the Mississippi River.

West Virginia is divided into three regions. These regions are the Appalachian Plateau, the Appalachian Ridge and Valley Region, and the Blue Ridge Region.

Appalachian Plateau

Much of West Virginia lies in the Appalachian Plateau. It covers 80 percent of the western part of the state. Forested

mountains make up this region. People mine coal and other natural resources in these mountains.

Many streams and rivers flow through the Appalachian Plateau. Many people live in large river valleys, like the Kanawha River Valley.

Appalachian Ridge and Valley Region

Eastern West Virginia lies within the heavily forested Appalachian Ridge and Valley Region. The Allegheny Mountains, part of the Appalachians, divide the Appalachian Plateau from the Ridge and Valley Region. The Allegheny Mountains include West Virginia's highest point, Spruce Knob. It is 4,861 feet (1,482 meters) above sea level.

The Allegheny Mountains are made of layered sedimentary rock. Erosion has worn away this soft rock, causing steep ridges and valleys to form. These ridges and valleys run northeast to southwest. Rivers, such as the Potomac, flow between the ridges.

Blue Ridge Region

The Blue Ridge Region is at the state's eastern tip. The Blue Ridge Mountains lie in the region. These mountains belong to the Appalachians.

West Virginia's Land Features

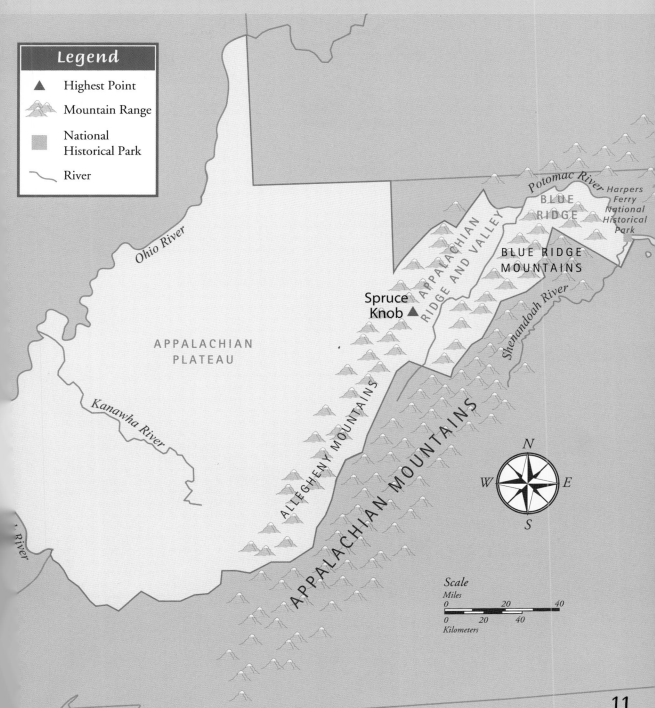

Legend

▲ Highest Point

Mountain Range

National Historical Park

River

Ohio River

Potomac River

BLUE RIDGE

Harpers Ferry National Historical Park

APPALACHIAN RIDGE AND VALLEY

BLUE RIDGE MOUNTAINS

Spruce Knob ▲

Shenandoah River

APPALACHIAN PLATEAU

Kanawha River

ALLEGHENY MOUNTAINS

APPALACHIAN MOUNTAINS

River

N
W   E
S

Scale
Miles
0   20   40
0   20   40
Kilometers

The Blue Ridge Region includes the Shenandoah and Potomac rivers. Some farmers grow fruit in the Shenandoah River Valley's fertile land. The state's lowest point is along the Potomac River at Harpers Ferry. It is 240 feet (73 meters) above sea level.

The Climate

West Virginia's average temperatures are 72 degrees Fahrenheit (22 degrees Celsius) during summer and 33 degrees Fahrenheit (1 degree Celsius) during winter. The temperatures in West Virginia vary according to regions. Temperatures usually are cooler in the mountains. They are warmer in the valleys.

West Virginia gets a great deal of precipitation. The state averages 44 inches (112 centimeters) each year. Most of the state's precipitation is rain, but snow is common in the mountains. The heaviest rainfall in the state occurs in the south. Some southern areas receive more than 50 inches (127 centimeters) of rain each year. The Potomac River Valley gets the least amount of rain.

Floods often happen in the state due to heavy rainfall. The lower river valleys may flood during winter and spring. In May 2002, a flood caused damage to the southern part of the state. More than 3,000 people were without power,

The Potomac River near Harpers Ferry is the state's lowest point.

The Cheat Mountain Salamander

The Cheat Mountain salamander lives only in West Virginia. This small amphibian is found in five counties. The Cheat Mountain salamander lives in moist red spruce forests where the ground is covered with fallen leaves, logs, and sticks. Adults are about 4 inches (10 centimeters) long. They are black or dark brown with copper or silver flecks on their backs.

Since the late 1980s, the Cheat Mountain salamander has been considered threatened. Threatened animals may soon become endangered. Habitat loss is the main reason for the salamander's status. Foresters cut down trees, causing sunlight to dry out the damp conditions the salamanders need to live. Scientists are keeping track of Cheat Mountain salamander populations. Recent records show that the number of salamanders remains steady.

and 7,400 people had no drinking water because of the flood. Hundreds of homes were destroyed and six people died.

Plants and Wildlife

Many plants grow in West Virginia's forests. Oak, cherry, maple, and other hardwood trees grow along the mountainsides. Softwood evergreen trees, including white pine, spruce, and hemlock, also grow in the area. Orchards of fruit trees and flowering trees like the dogwood thrive in river valleys. Rhododendrons grow throughout the state. Their flower clusters range in color from white to purple.

Many animals live in West Virginia. Black bears, white-tailed deer, bobcats, raccoons, and skunks roam West Virginia's forests. Cardinals, quail, grouse, and many other birds also make their home in the state.

Some of West Virginia's animals are endangered. These animals may soon die out. They include the Cheat Mountain salamander, the West Virginia northern flying squirrel, the Virginia big-eared bat, and the Indiana bat.

Mound Builders built the Grave Creek Mou
thousands of years ago. Today, it is part of
national historic site.

Chapter 3

History of West Virginia

About 3,000 years ago, native people called the Mound Builders lived in West Virginia. The Mound Builders buried their dead leaders in large dirt mounds. The largest mound is in the town of Moundsville. Known as the Grave Creek Mound, it is 69 feet (21 meters) tall.

In the 1600s, Shawnee and Delaware Indians hunted and fished in present-day West Virginia. They made many trails through the area. Other hunters and traders continued to use these trails. Some of the trails even became modern highways.

Colonists started the first permanent settlement in Jamestown, Virginia, in 1607.

First Explorers and Settlers

In the early 1600s, England formed colonies on the eastern coast of North America. England later became part of Great Britain. In 1607, a group of English colonists settled in Virginia. In 1624, King James I officially made Virginia an English colony.

In 1671, Englishmen Thomas Batts and Robert Fallam explored the area that became southern West Virginia. Fur trader Abraham Wood hired the men. Fur traders trapped animals and then traded or sold the skins. Wood wanted to become well known in the fur trade. The fur trade was a good way to make money. Batts and Fallam found a river that flowed west, unlike most other area rivers that flowed east. They named it Wood's River, later called the New River. England claimed the area after the expedition.

In the early 1700s, colonists moved into areas of present-day West Virginia. In 1727, a group of Germans from Pennsylvania founded the town of Mecklenburg near the Potomac River. Today, the city is called Sheperdstown. About 1731, a Welshman named Morgan Morgan settled near the present-day town of Bunker Hill.

Wars

As British colonists settled in North America, they had problems with the French. Both France and Great Britain wanted to control the Ohio Territory. The territory included all of the land drained by the Ohio River and part of present-day West Virginia.

The struggle for land led to a war between the two countries. The war was called the French and Indian War (1754–1763). Many of the war's battles occurred in western Virginia. Great

Britain won the war. After the war, France gave all of its claims to North America to Britain. Great Britain now controlled the land west of the Appalachian Mountains all the way to the Mississippi River.

Those who fought in the French and Indian War crossed over the rough land of the Appalachian Mountains. Both France and Britain wanted control of this area.

By the mid-1700s, colonists felt Great Britain was treating them unfairly. The colonists wanted independence from Great Britain. In 1775, the Revolutionary War (1775–1783) began. Fort Henry, which is present-day Wheeling, was attacked by the British and American Indians twice. In the 1777 attack, many cabins were destroyed and cattle were killed. In 1782, the colonists defended the fort and the attackers gave up their fight. The colonists won the war after many hard battles. The United States finally gained its independence.

Settlement and Conflicts

After the Revolutionary War, many people came to live in present-day West Virginia. By 1790, more than 50,000 people lived there. By 1810, this number doubled.

People began to find and use the natural resources in western Virginia. Businesses manufactured salt near the Kanawha River Valley. Coal mining businesses supplied coal to the salt producers. The salt companies used the coal as fuel to heat their furnaces.

Many settlers in western Virginia felt they were treated unfairly by the state of Virginia and the federal government. They did not like Virginia's policy on property taxes. Men had to own a certain amount of land to have the right to vote.

Many people in western Virginia could not vote because they rented land or did not own enough land. The eastern counties had more representation in the legislature. More people lived in these areas.

Western and eastern Virginians felt differently about slavery. Many Virginian slaves worked on farms and in the salt and coal mines. Most easterners supported slavery. Some western Virginians disagreed with it. Fewer people in western Virginia owned slaves than in other parts of the state.

Western Virginians tried to solve disagreements with the government. They held constitutional conventions in 1829 and 1850. In 1850, they settled some of the voting and legislature issues. But conflicts between the eastern and western parts of the state continued.

Raid on Harpers Ferry

The issue of slavery divided people not only in Virginia, but also throughout the United States. Some people, called abolitionists, wanted to end slavery. Sometimes these people went to great lengths to fight for their cause. On October 16, 1859, abolitionist John Brown and a group of men raided a federal armory in Harpers Ferry, located in present-day West Virginia.

A group of soldiers captured John Brown after his raid on a federal weapons storehouse.

A group of soldiers led by Lieutenant Colonel Robert E. Lee captured Brown and his men. A number of Virginians and some of the raiders died. Brown's sons Watson and Oliver died in the raid. Brown's other son, Owen, and several others escaped. Brown was tried in court for treason against the state of Virginia. He was sentenced to death. In December, John Brown was hanged in Charles Town.

The raid on Harpers Ferry made more people aware of slavery issues. It also caused problems between those for and against slavery.

The Civil War and Statehood

In 1861, the Civil War (1861–1865) began after some southern states seceded from, or left, the United States. They formed the Confederate States of America. Virginia decided to join the newly-formed Confederacy. But the western counties voted to stay with the Union.

Five days after the Civil War began, a group of people living in western Virginia voted to secede from the state. They wanted to name their new state Kanawha. But Kanawha was dropped in favor of West Virginia during the writing of the state constitution. In April 1862, West Virginia's residents approved the constitution. On June 20, 1863, West Virginia became the 35th state.

Many Civil War battles occurred in West Virginia. One of the most important battles was the Battle of Harpers Ferry in September 1862. More Union troops surrendered there than during any other Civil War battle.

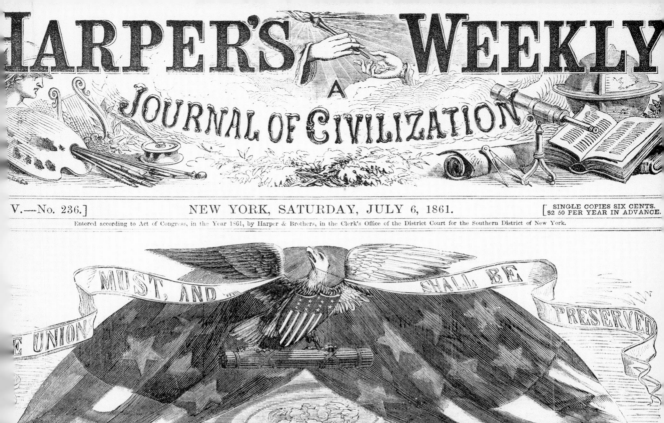

HARPER'S WEEKLY

A
JOURNAL OF CIVILIZATION

V.—No. 236.] NEW YORK, SATURDAY, JULY 6, 1861. [SINGLE COPIES SIX CENTS.
[$2 50 PER YEAR IN ADVANCE.

Entered according to Act of Congress, in the Year 1861, by Harper & Brothers, in the Clerk's Office of the District Court for the Southern District of New York.

Magazines and newspapers wrote about conventions in Wheeling. People opposing the state's secession attended these conventions.

Miners worked long hours in the dirty coal mines of West Virginia. Sometimes miners went on strike to try to improve their working conditions.

The Early 1900s

After the Civil War, the economy in West Virginia improved. Workers found jobs building railroads throughout the state to transport coal and timber. West Virginians started finding more uses for state's oil and natural gas resources.

"In West Virginia, it [coal] is the staff of life. The state is a huge layercake, hacked into great slices by the elements; the slices are mountains, the layers are rocks, and the filling is coal."
—James M. Cain, author of These United States, *1924*

In the early 1900s, many West Virginians worked in coal mines. The work was dangerous. The mines had little fresh air flowing through them. Many people developed lung problems. Explosions sometimes killed workers. In 1907, the worst coal mining explosion in the nation's history happened in Monongah. More than 360 people died.

Some miners were angry about their working conditions and poor wages. They formed labor unions to try to solve these problems. West Virginian coal miners made less money than miners in other states. Unions sometimes went on strike, or stopped working, when company owners refused to improve working conditions or wages.

The U.S. economy suffered during the Great Depression (1929–1939). Many people in West Virginia and around the country lost their jobs. Coal production went down. More people were unemployed in West Virginia than in many other states. The U.S. government gave money, created jobs, and started programs to help the unemployed.

Recent Times

World War II (1939–1945) helped bring the country out of the Depression. West Virginians made steel for military equipment. They mined coal to power factories.

New machines for farming and coal mining became available during the 1950s. Fewer workers were needed to perform jobs. The coal market also declined. Many homes and businesses switched from coal to oil for heating. Young people could not find work. They left the state. From 1950 to 1970, the state's population dropped 13 percent.

During the 1960s and 1970s, West Virginia's economy improved. The federal government gave the state money to create jobs. Many people went to work building highways across the state. The government also encouraged new businesses to open. An energy crisis and oil shortage in the 1970s caused many people and businesses to start using coal for fuel again.

West Virginia's economy grew throughout the 1990s. Coal production increased. Electricity-generating plants worked to meet the needs of a growing population. Tourism and other service industries brought new jobs to the state.

Chuck Yeager

uring the early 1940s, most people
elieved that it was impossible to fly
ster than the speed of sound. But test
lot Charles "Chuck" Yeager proved
em wrong.

Yeager was born February 13, 1923,
Myra, West Virginia, and grew up in
amlin. He joined the Army Air Corps in
942 and flew fighter aircraft in World
ar II. After the war, he was selected to
lp test a new rocket-powered plane
lled the X-1. On October 14, 1947,
ager flew the X-1 and broke the
und barrier.

Yeager trained new test pilots and also
w missions during the Vietnam War
954–1975). He retired from active
ilitary duty in 1975.

Throughout his career, Yeager earned
any awards and honors, including the
esidential Medal of Freedom and the rank
brigadier general.

West Virginia's state capitol building in Charleston houses many state government offices.

Chapter 4

Government and Politics

West Virginia became a state in 1863. The state approved its first constitution that same year. In 1875, West Virginia adopted a new constitution. This constitution is still in effect today. It has been amended, or changed, more than 50 times.

Branches of Government

Under West Virginia's constitution, the government is divided into the executive, legislative, and judicial branches. The executive branch carries out laws. The governor is the head of the executive branch. The governor is elected to four-year terms, and can serve no more than two terms in a row. The governor can pass or veto the laws the legislative branch makes. Other elected officers of this branch include the secretary of state, the state auditor, and the attorney general.

The legislative branch makes state laws. The senate and the house of delegates make up the legislature. The senate includes 34 members. Voters elect them to four-year terms. The house of delegates has 100 members. These members are elected to two-year terms.

West Virginia's judicial branch interprets the state's laws. This branch includes magistrate courts, circuit courts, family courts, and the supreme court of appeals. West Virginia has 158 magistrate courts. Magistrate courts hear minor criminal and civil cases involving less than $5,000. More serious crimes and civil cases involving more than $5,000 must be heard in circuit courts. In 2002, West Virginia created family courts. Family courts hear cases involving child custody, divorce, and other family matters.

The supreme court of appeals is the highest court in West Virginia. It hears cases that have been appealed. Cases

West Virginia's Government

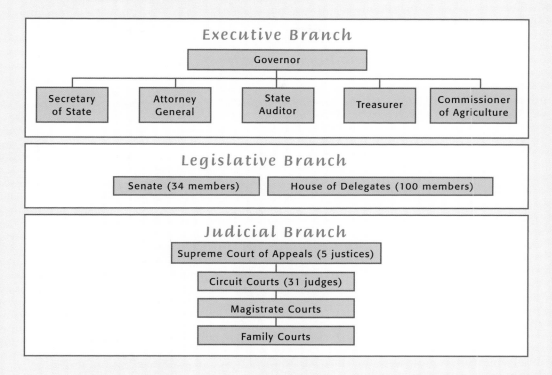

Executive Branch

Governor

Secretary of State | Attorney General | State Auditor | Treasurer | Commissioner of Agriculture

Legislative Branch

Senate (34 members) | House of Delegates (100 members)

Judicial Branch

Supreme Court of Appeals (5 justices)

Circuit Courts (31 judges)

Magistrate Courts

Family Courts

on appeal have already been decided by a lower court. When one of the parties involved in a case appeals a ruling, they ask to have the case reviewed by another court. The supreme court of appeals also decides whether state laws are legal according to the state constitution. The supreme court's five justices are elected to 12-year terms.

Cyrus Vance often spoke about his ideas to other members of the U.S. Congress. He played an important role in international politics while serving as secretary of state from 1977 to 1980.

West Virginia Politics

West Virginians vote for both Republicans and Democrats in elections. Democratic presidential candidates have been chosen more often than Republican candidates over the last several decades.

Some West Virginians have had major roles in national politics. Current U.S. Senator Robert C. Byrd has served longer in the U.S. Senate than any other West Virginian. Byrd was elected to the Senate in 1958. Only three members of Congress have served longer than Byrd. Byrd has held many leadership positions, including chair of the Senate Appropriations Committee and Democratic Majority and Minority leader.

West Virginian Cyrus Vance was U.S. secretary of state from 1977 to 1980. He worked to improve international relations. In 1992, Vance went on a peace mission to Yugoslavia. He died in 2002.

The Sunset Law

West Virginians passed the Sunset Law to make sure their government runs smoothly. This law makes sure all members of state agencies and commissions are doing their jobs correctly. Under the Sunset Law, workers in each agency must report their accomplishments. The state legislature's Performance Evaluation and Research Division studies each agency's records every year. The division then reports to a legislative committee. The committee decides whether the agency is doing its job correctly. If the committee decides the agency is not doing its job, the agency may not be allowed to continue.

Strip mining has replaced
underground coal mining
in some parts of the state.

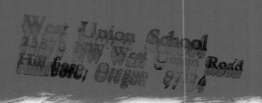

Economy and Resources

West Virginia depends on coal mining as an important source of income. But coal mining is less important to the economy than it once was. Today, service, manufacturing, and other industries also support the state's economy.

Service Industries

Most of West Virginia's income comes from service industries. People in service industries work in many settings. Some work in hotels and restaurants. The service industry also includes government, hospital, and education workers.

The state of West Virginia works to encourage tourism. Today, it is the state's leading industry. Visitors hike in the state's forests and parks. Rock climbers explore West Virginia's mountains. Whitewater rafters float down West Virginia's fast-flowing rivers. Many whitewater rafters travel on the New River and Gauley River.

Mining

Coal is one of West Virginia's greatest natural resources. West Virginia produces about 15 percent of the country's coal. It also produces almost half of the coal that the United States sells to other countries. Today, fewer people use coal to heat their homes than they did in the past. Instead, power plants use coal

to make electricity. Coal is the main source of electricity in 32 states. It provides more than 50 percent of the country's electricity.

From 1970 to 1997, the number of mining jobs went down by 45 percent. Many miners lost their jobs after they were replaced by machines. The decrease in mining jobs and a lack of other jobs forced people to leave the state. From 1990 to 2000, the state's population grew less than one percent.

The state can no longer rely on coal as much as it once did. The state government has created programs to attract new businesses and

Whitewater rafting is a popular sport on the Gauley River. Experienced rafters ride the fast-moving Pillow Rock rapids.

help them grow. The state also encourages county and city governments to work together. By combining resources, governments can provide more opportunities for new businesses to grow.

West Virginia also produces other natural resources besides coal. Salt, natural gas, and oil can be found in the state. Most of the state's salt deposits are in the northern and north-central parts of the state. In recent years, natural gas production has reached about 200,000 million cubic feet (5,660 million cubic meters). Many of the natural gas fields are in the western part of the state. In 1999, the state produced about 1.5 million barrels of oil. Workers also mine sand, gravel, and clay.

Manufacturing

West Virginia's natural resources have helped major manufacturing companies grow. The Kanawha River Valley is home to many chemical companies. Ninety-five percent of the state's salt is used to make chlorine. Chlorine is a chemical used in some cleaning supplies. It is also used to make plastic and other materials. Wheeling is an important center for steel manufacturing.

Blenko Glass workers use various tools to help them form their famous handblown glassware.

Glass and pottery makers depend on the state's supplies of sand and clay. One of the world's leading stained-glass makers, Blenko Glass, is based in Milton. William Blenko started the company in 1921. The company makes decorative pieces, vases, and other glassware. Blenko Glass has also supplied glass for the windows of many famous buildings, including Westminster Abbey in London, England, and the White House in Washington, D.C.

Agriculture and Forestry

Only about 6 percent of West Virginia is farmland. Beef cattle are the state's most valuable farm product. Farmers also raise dairy cattle, chickens, and turkeys. They grow corn, barley, wheat, oats, and soybeans. Fruit growers raise apples, peaches, grapes, and berries. West Virginia ranks ninth in the nation in apple production. Apple growers produce about 115 million pounds (52 million kilograms) of apples each year.

Many valuable hardwood trees such as oak and cherry grow in West Virginia's forests. Forests that cover the mountains give the state a large supply of wood. Foresters cut the trees into logs. Then the logs are milled into lumber. Lumber from hardwood trees is strong and durable. People use the lumber in many homes and businesses. The forestry industry provides about $2.1 billion to West Virginia's economy each year.

Beef cattle graze in a West Virginia field surrounded by mountains. Beef and dairy cattle are important agricultural resources in West Virginia.

The Apple Butter Festival in Berkeley Springs draws many visitors each year.

44

Chapter 6

People and Culture

West Virginia has a population of about 2 million. Most West Virginians live in rural areas. West Virginia's largest cities are small compared to the largest cities in many other states. Some of the state's most heavily populated counties are in the east. Charleston, West Virginia's capital, is the state's largest city.

The People

Many West Virginians have European backgrounds. The first settlers who came to West Virginia were German, English, Welsh, and Scottish. Other Europeans, including

West Virginia's Ethnic Backgrounds

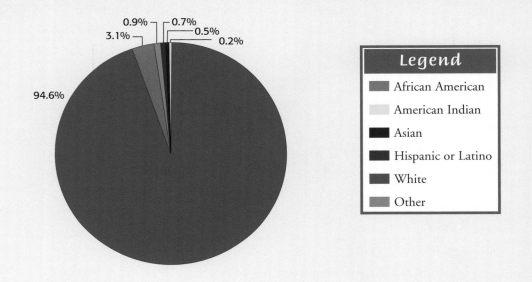

0.9%
3.1%
0.7%
0.5%
0.2%
94.6%

Legend
- African American
- American Indian
- Asian
- Hispanic or Latino
- White
- Other

Russians, Hungarians, Italians, and Poles, came after the Civil War. Many of these people came to work at the state's railroad companies, coal mines, and logging camps.

Few minorities live in West Virginia. African Americans make up just more than 3 percent of the state's population. Only 0.5 percent of the state's residents are Asian.

Festivals and Food

West Virginians have a rich cultural background in music and art. They hold folk festivals each year. Many folk songs have their roots in Irish, Scottish, and English music. Folk festivals often include fiddling contests, ballad singing, and the handcrafting of furniture and instruments.

Other gatherings mark important times in West Virginia's past. Residents celebrate Civil War Days in Gauley Bridge and the Blue and Gray Reunion in Philipi each year. At these festivals, West Virginians remember how the Civil War

Some West Virginians reenact important historical events.

affected their state. The West Virginia Oil and Gas Festival is celebrated each year in Sistersville. People learn about the history of West Virginia's oil and natural gas industries at this festival.

West Virginians enjoy many foods. Some traditional West Virginia foods are deep-fried ramps and pawpaws. Ramps are a type of onion that grow in West Virginia's mountains in spring. Ramp festivals are held throughout the state each year. Outdoor markets sometimes sell pawpaws, a type of fruit. Many orchards around the state grow apples. West Virginians use pawpaws and apples in pies and other desserts.

Education

West Virginia's schools work hard to educate the state's children. Many schools are small. Small schools allow teachers to work with students more closely. School officials try to provide students with new computers and the most recent equipment. Recently, the state has made more college scholarships available to high school students.

After students graduate from high school, some choose to study at colleges in the state. These colleges include West Virginia University, Marshall University, and the West Virginia University Institute of Technology.

Apple trees bloom before apples start to grow on their branches. The apple blossoms smell sweet.

Pearl S. Buck

Writer Pearl S. Buck was born in Hillsboro, West Virginia, in 1892. Her parents were missionaries. They took Pearl with them when they went to China. She lived in China for 40 years before coming back to the United States. In 1938, Buck won the Nobel Prize for Literature, one of the highest honors a writer can receive. She was the first American woman to receive this honor.

Buck wrote more than 70 books. One of her best-known books, *The Good Earth*, is the story of a young woman growing up in China. It won the Pulitzer Prize in 1935. Pearl S. Buck died in 1973.

In addition to the public school system, the state works to encourage community education. West Virginia currently has over 170 public library systems. Bookmobiles also travel to rural areas, making books available to people of all ages. Public TV and radio stations bring educational programs to the state.

Writers

Several famous writers have come from West Virginia. Pearl S. Buck and Walter Dean Myers became authors of popular books for young people. One of Buck's novels, *The Good Earth*, was made into a movie. Myers' book, *Somewhere in the Darkness*, won a Newbery honor in 1993. The book also received other honors and awards.

Sports

West Virginia does not have any professional sports teams. But many famous athletes have come from West Virginia. They include baseball player George Brett and basketball player Jerry West. George Brett was inducted into the National Baseball Hall of Fame in 1999. Jerry West held many records while playing with the Los Angeles Lakers from 1960 to 1974. His silhouette is featured in the NBA logo. Mary Lou Retton, a gymnast from West Virginia, won an Olympic gold medal in 1984.

Musicians and Performers

West Virginia has a strong background in music and the performing arts. *Jamboree USA*, in Wheeling, is one of the longest-running live radio shows in the nation. Modern country music stars such as Randy Travis, Alan Jackson, and West Virginia native Kathy Mattea have performed there. Actor Don Knotts grew up in Morgantown. He was a star on the *Andy Griffith Show*, a popular TV series of the 1960s. Many movies have also been filmed in West Virginia.

Perceptions

West Virginia is rich in history and culture. Because of West Virginia's many rural citizens, people in other states sometimes think West Virginians are uneducated and unfamiliar with lifestyles outside of their state. But West Virginians are proud of their state and its growing economic and educational opportunities. They work hard to make West Virginia a place for residents and tourists to enjoy.

Recipe: Black Walnut Maple Pie

The main ingredients in this recipe come from trees in West Virginia. West Virginia's official state tree, the sugar maple, grows throughout the state. Black walnut trees are also common in the forests of West Virginia.

Ingredients

2 eggs
1 cup (240 mL) brown sugar
2 tablespoons (30 mL) flour
3 tablespoons (45 mL) butter
    or margarine
2 teaspoons (10 mL) cinnamon
1 cup (240 mL) maple syrup
1 teaspoon (5 mL) vanilla
1 cup (240 mL) chopped
    black walnuts
1 9-inch (23-centimeter)
    prepared pie crust with pan

Equipment

large mixing bowl
electric mixer
mixing spoon
oven mitts

What You Do

1. Preheat oven to 375°F (190°C).

2. In a large mixing bowl, beat eggs with mixer until fluffy. Add sugar, flour, butter, and cinnamon. Beat until creamy.

3. Stir in syrup, vanilla, and walnuts. Pour mixture into pie crust.

4. Bake for 30 to 45 minutes.

5. Remove from oven with oven mitts. Let cool and serve.

Makes 6 to 8 servings

West Virginia's Flag and Seal

West Virginia's Flag

West Virginia's state flag was adopted in 1929. The state seal is featured on a white background. The rhododendron, the state flower, surrounds the seal. A blue border surrounds the flag.

West Virginia's State Seal

The state seal features a farmer and a miner standing next to a rock. West Virginia's date of statehood, June 20, 1863, is on the rock. Rifles are near the seal's bottom. The Cap of Liberty, a symbol of freedom, lies on top of the rifles. The state motto, "Montani semper liberi," is written under the rifles. It means "Mountaineers are always free."

Almanac

General Facts

Nicknames: Mountain State, Panhandle State

Population: 1,808,344
Population rank: 37th

Capital: Charleston

Largest cities: Charleston, Huntington, Parkersburg, Morgantown, Weirton

Agriculture

Agricultural products: cattle, poultry, corn, wheat, soybeans, fruit

Climate

Average summer temperature: 72 degrees Fahrenheit (22 degrees Celsius)

Average winter temperature: 33 degrees Fahrenheit (1 degree Celsius)

Average annual precipitation: 44 inches (112 centimeters)

Geography

Area: 24,231 square miles (62,758 square kilometers)
Size rank: 41

Highest Point: Spruce Knob, 4,861 feet (1,482 meters) above sea level

Lowest Point: Potomac River, 240 feet (73 meters) above sea level

Monarch butterfly

Black bear

Economy

Natural Resources: Coal, natural gas, oil, salt, clay, sand, gravel

Types of Industry: Service, mining, chemical manufacturing, trade

Government

First governor: Arthur Boreman, 1863–1869

Statehood: June 20, 1863; 35th state

U.S. Representatives: 3

U.S. Senators: 2

U.S. electoral votes: 5

Counties: 55

Symbols

State animal: Black bear

State bird: Cardinal

State flower: Rhododendron

State fruit: Golden Delicious apple

Symbols

State insect: Monarch butterfly

State song: "The West Virginia Hills," by Reverend David King and H. E. Engle

State tree: Sugar maple

Timeline

State History

1671
Englishmen Thomas Batts and Robert Fallam travel to southern West Virginia.

1731
Welshman Morgan Morgan settles near present-day Bunker Hill.

1859
The raid of Harpers Ferry increases tensio between pro-slavery a anti-slavery activists.

U.S. History

1620
The Pilgrims establish a colony in North America.

1775–1783
American colonists and the British fight the Revolutionary War.

1861–1865
The Union and the Confederacy fight the Civil War.

1863

West Virginia becomes a state on June 20.

1907

At least 360 people die in a coal mine explosion in Monongah, making it the worst coal mine disaster in U.S. history.

1958

West Virginian Robert C. Byrd is elected to the U.S. Senate.

2002

A major flood in May causes severe damage to southern West Virginia.

1914–1918

World War I is fought; the United States enters the war in 1917.

1929–1939

The United States experiences the Great Depression.

1939–1945

World War II is fought; the United States enters the war in 1941.

1964

The U.S. Congress passes the Civil Rights Act, which makes discrimination illegal.

2001

On September 11, terrorists attack the World Trade Center and the Pentagon.

Words to Know

abolitionist (ab-uh-LISH-uh-nist)—someone who worked to end slavery before the Civil War

bookmobile (BUK-moh-beel)—a large van or bus that carries library books

coal (KOHL)—a black mineral formed from the remains of ancient plants

colony (KOL-uh-nee)—an area where people from another country have settled

erosion (e-ROH-zhuhn)—the wearing away of land by water or wind

legislature (LEJ-iss-lay-chur)—a group of people elected to make laws

secede (si-SEED)—to formally withdraw from a group; people in western Virginia voted to secede from the state in 1861.

sedimentary rock (sed-uh-MEN-tuh-ree ROK)—rock that is formed by layers of rocks, sand, or dirt that has been pressed together

strike (STRIKE)—to refuse to work because of a disagreement with the employer over wages or working conditions

To Learn More

Becker, Helaine. *John Brown.* The Civil War. Woodbridge, Conn.: Blackbirch Press, 2001.

Di Piazza, Domenica. *West Virginia.* Hello U.S.A. Minneapolis: Lerner, 2002.

Fazio, Wende. *West Virginia.* America the Beautiful. New York: Children's Press, 2000.

Hoffman, Nancy. *West Virginia.* Celebrate the States. New York: Benchmark Books, 1999.

Internet Sites

Do you want to find out more about West Virginia?
Let FactHound, our fact-finding hound dog, do the research for you.

Here's how:
1) Visit ***http://www.facthound.com***
2) Type in the **Book ID** number:
   0736822054
3) Click on **FETCH IT**.

FactHound will fetch Internet sites picked by our editors just for you!

Places to Write and Visit

The Cultural Center
1900 Kanawha Boulevard East
Charleston, WV 25305–0300

Harpers Ferry National Historical Park
P.O. Box 65
Harpers Ferry, WV 25425

Secretary of State
Building 1, Suite 157-K
1900 Kanawha Boulevard East
Charleston, WV 25305-0770

West Virginia Capitol Complex
1900 Kanawha Boulevard
Charleston, WV 25305

West Virginia Division of Tourism
90 MacCorkle Avenue South West
South Charleston, WV 25303

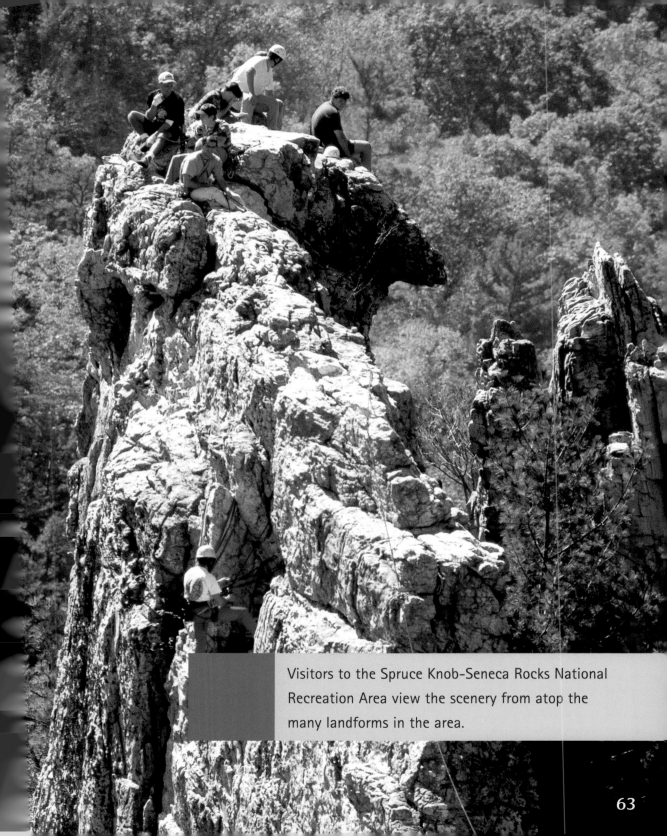

Visitors to the Spruce Knob-Seneca Rocks National Recreation Area view the scenery from atop the many landforms in the area.

Index

West Union School
23870 NW West Union Road
Hillsboro, Oregon 97124

T 57067